Hand in Hand with the Master

31 Devotions

Moments to Remind You of God's Love

Merle M. Mills

ISBN 13:978-0-9886 162-0-2

Scripture quotations noted KJV are taken from the Holy Bible, King James Version.

Scripture quotations noted NIV are taken from the Holy Bible, New International Version ®. NIV ®.Copyright © 1973, 1978, 1984 by International Bible Society. Used by permission of Zondervan Publishing House. All rights reserved.

Scripture quotations noted NLT are taken from the Holy Bible, New Living Translation, copyright © 1996, 2004. Used by permission of Tyndale House Publishers, Inc., Wheaton, Illinois 60189. All rights reserved.

www.changedthrutheword.org
www.nomoreasecret.blogspot.com

Cover and Interior Design by Evelyn J. Wagoner

Preface

My extensive search for peace and wholeness led to the pages of the Holy Scriptures. There I discovered promises offering forgiveness from the past and hope for my future. My life changed from pain to peace ... depression to joy ... weakness to strength.

I guarantee that if you commit yourself to reading the Word every day, memorizing it, you too will experience a changed life.

Merle M. Mills

Dedication

To Roosevelt Rolle . . . thank you for inspiring me to step out in faith and equip women through the Word. Now it's your turn to use your God-given gift and, as Wordsworth said, *"fill your paper with the breathings of your heart . . ."*

To my family . . . thank you for supporting me by giving me the freedom of hours at my computer. You're allowing me to fulfill my passion to write and to minister God's extravagant love—to help others join me on this great journey to peace . . . to joy . . . to strength.

And to my God—thank You for loving me. As long as You give me breath, I will serve You.

Merle M. Mills

Contents

DAY 1

Look Up

Throughout the day,
I often
find it necessary
to stop in the midst
of an overwhelming moment
and look up
to the Great Creator.

Then a calming effect takes place
as I remember
I am not alone
to continue the tasks ahead.

"I lift up my eyes to the hills—
where does my help come from?
My help comes from the LORD,
the Maker of heaven and earth."
                    ~ Psalm 121:1-2 (NIV)

Day 2

A Prayer for Today

Heavenly Father,
Help me not to worry about anything,
but in every situation to ask You
for what I need in prayer
and then give thanks
to You.
Then Your peace,
which goes beyond anything I can imagine,
will guard my thoughts and emotions
through Christ Jesus.
So why should I worry
when You are able
through Your power
to do infinitely
more than I have asked or imagined?
In Jesus' name,
Amen!

Philippians 4:6-7; Ephesians 3:20

DAY 3

Valued

The beauty of nature
blue skies
wild rabbits
waterfalls
trees
flowers
birds
mountains.

To the Great Creator, you and I are of much
more value than all of these!

"And the very hairs on your head are all
numbered. So don't be afraid; you are more
valuable to God than a whole flock of sparrows."
~ Luke 12:7 (NLT)

Day 4

My Prayer for You

That you will not be afraid
because God has not given you
the spirit of fear;
but of power, and of love,
and of a sound mind.[1]
That you will know that He loves you
with an everlasting love.[2]
That will understand that you are precious
in His sight.[3]
That you will experience His peace,
which exceeds anything you can
understand.[4]
This is my prayer for you.
In Jesus' name,
Amen!

[1] *2 Timothy 1:7*
[2] *Jeremiah 31:3*
[3] *Isaiah 43:4*
[4] *Philippians 4:7*

Day 5

Forgiven

Our subconscious mind "has the ability to record and remember every incident that it experiences."[1] This may be one of the reasons why we sometimes have difficulty forgetting our sin. Whatever the past sin is that we are trying to forget, somehow the memory not only lingers, but hinders our daily living and our relationship with God.

However, we do have a hope ... precious promises from the pages of Scripture: If we confess our sins, He is faithful and just and will forgive us our sins and purify us from all unrighteousness.[2] *"For I am merciful. I will not keep anger forever*[3] *... I will never again remember your sins.*[4] These words have inbuilt, thought-changing power to help us move into hope and live beyond guilt. I dared to believe them. Will you?

---

[1] *studentstepstosuccess.com/index.php;*
[2] *1 John 1:9*
[3] *Jeremiah 3:12b*
[4] *Hebrews 8:12b*

Day 6

A Prayer for Secret Fears

Heavenly Father,
at times
I secretly fear.
Thank You
that
during those times
You shine
Your light
on those secret fears
and
I become
fearless.

"When I am afraid, I put my trust in You." ~ Psalm 56:3 (NIV)

"I prayed to the Lord, and He answered me. He freed me from all my fears." ~ Psalm 34:4 (NLT)

Day 7

I Ask

Heavenly Father,
I ask today
for wisdom.
I ask today
for peace.
I ask today
that You
wipe away
my tears
and fill me
with Your
joy!

*"You have turned my mourning into joyful
dancing. You have taken away my clothes of
mourning and clothed me with joy,"*
                                        ~ Psalm 30:11 (NLT)

"They that sow in tears shall reap in joy."
                                        ~ Psalm 126:5 (KJV)

Day 8

*A Prayer
from the Psalms*

Heavenly Father,
Today, lead me beside
the still waters, [1]
guide me with Your eye,[2]
and set my feet on a rock.[3]
In Jesus' name,
Amen!

[1]*Psalm 23:2*
[2]*Psalm 32:8*
[3]*Psalm 40:2*

Day 9

The Greatest Offer

"Come now, and let us reason together, says the LORD: though your sins be as scarlet, they shall be as white as snow; though they be red like crimson, they shall be as wool."[1]

"I will forgive your iniquity, and I will remember your sin no more!"[2]

The offer is for you and for me. I accepted it, and never for one moment have I regretted it—never for one moment!

[1] *Isaiah 1:18*
[2] *Jeremiah 31:34b*

Day 10

A Daily Appointment

Exclusive Daily Appointment
at the Master's Feet

It teaches me that I am loved
—and how to love others. [1]
It teaches me that I am forgiven
—and how to forgive others. [2]
It teaches me wisdom
—and how to share this wisdom with others. [3]
It teaches me how to pray and receive
answers for myself—and for others. [4]
It is the most vital part of my day!

Have you had your appointment with the
Master today?

[1] *John 13:34*
[2] *Ephesians 4:32*
[3] *Psalms 111:10*
[4] *James 5:16*

Day 11

Change of Name

Holy[1]
Accepted[2]
Redeemed[3]
Precious[4]
Honorable[5]
Apple[6]
Special[7]

These names are always available and sure beat some that I have been called, or that I have called myself. I am ready for the change. How about you?

[1] *Ephesians 1:4*
[2] *Ephesians 1:6*
[3] *Isaiah 43:1*
[4,5] *Isaiah 43:4*
[6] *Zechariah 2:8b*
[7] *Deuteronomy 7:6*

Day 12

The Cross

The greatest symbol of love
the world will ever see![1]
The greatest demonstration of love
the world will ever need![2]
The greatest commitment of love
you or I will ever make![3]
Father, thank You for the cross,
its love-changing,
love-giving,
and love-sustaining power.
In Jesus' name,
Amen.

[1] *John 15:13*
[2] *Romans 5:8*
[3] *Philippians 3:10*

Day 13

A Blessing

I pray that you will be aware of God's eternal love surrounding you today, as you go about your daily activities.[1]

I pray that you will give all your worries and cares to Him, because He cares about what happens to you.[2]

I pray that you will not let your heart be troubled.[3]

I pray that the Lord will bless you and keep you; make His face shine upon you, and be gracious unto you; I pray that the Lord show you His favor, and give you His peace.[4]

In Jesus' name, Amen!

[1] *Exodus 33:14*
[2] *Peter 5:7*
[3] *John 14:1*
[4] *Numbers 6:24-26*

Day 14

The Greatest Specialist

The Greatest Specialist's
cures for the following:
Anxiety[1]
Broken Hearts[2]
Depression[3]
Fainting[4]
Tears[5]
Weakness[6]
Weariness[7]

Accepting new patients
No appointment necessary
Many references available
Call today: 1-The-Holy-Bible

[1] *Philippians 4:6*
[2] *Luke 4:18*
[3] *Psalm 42:5/11*
[4] *Isaiah 40:29*
[5] *Psalm 116:8*
[6] *Job 26:2*
[7] *Matthew 11:28*

Day 15

The Name

The Name that has the ability:
... to heal[1] ... to forgive[2]
    ... to give peace[3] ... to comfort[4]
        ... to answer prayer[5]
            ... to protect[6]
                ... to strengthen[7]
                    ... to provide [8]
                        ... to give hope.[9]
I call the Name often.
Jesus. ...
Jesus.
Jesus!

[1] *Psalm 103:3*
[2] *Micah 7:19*
[3] *Psalm 29:11*
[4] *Psalm 23:4*
[5] *Isaiah 65:24*
[6] *Psalm 91:7*
[7] *Psalm 37:39*
[8] *Psalm 37:25*
[9] *Psalm 71:5*

Day 16

The Greatest Companion

"I will guide you along the best pathway
for your life.[1]
I will advise you and watch over you.[2]
I will be with you in trouble.[3]
I will be with you through fiery trials.[4]
I will uphold you.[5]
I never sleep,[6] so why not go ahead and
let me give you, My beloved, sweet sleep?[7]
I will never leave you.[8]
I will never forsake you.[9]
I am with you to the end of the world."[10]

~ Jesus

[1] *Psalm 32:8a*
[2] *Psalm 32:8b*
[3] *Psalm 91:15b*
[4] *Isaiah 43:2c*
[5] *Isaiah 41:10c*
[6] *Psalm 121:4*
[7] *Psalm 127:2*
[8,9] *Hebrews 13:5*
[10] *Matthew 28:20b*

Day 17

The Greatest Love

I have set My love upon you.[1]
My love for you passes knowledge.[2]
I think of you often.[3]
You are of value to Me.[4]
You are the apple of My eye.[5]

Will You be mine?[6]
I gave My life for you.[7]
I love you unconditionally.[8] ...
I love you forever![9]

~ Jesus

[1] *Psalm 91:14*
[2] *Ephesians 3:19*
[3] *Psalm 139:17-18*
[4] *Luke 12:7b*
[5] *Zechariah 2:8b*
[6] *Isaiah 43:1*
[7] *John 3:16*
[8] *Romans 8:38-39*
[9] *Jeremiah 31:3*

Day 18

Ask

For joy[1]
peace[2]
comfort[3]
forgiveness[4]
strength[5]
hope[6]
love[7] ...

REQUIREMENT:
Ask,[8]
then believe![9]

[1] *Psalm 16:11*
[2] *John 14:27*
[3] *Isaiah 61:2*
[4] *Psalm 103:3*
[5] *Psalm 27:1*
[6] *Psalm 39:7*
[7] *John 3:16*
[8] *Matthew 7:9*
[9] *Mark 11:24*

Day 19

Now

Heavenly Father,
help me
to be patient
to be kind—
now.
To laugh
to forgive—
now.
To enjoy
fully
the gift of life
that You have given me—
now!

"Behold, now is the accepted time;
behold, now is the day of salvation."
                    ~ 2 Corinthians 6:2 (NJKV)

Day 20

Amazed

That you would
    Forgive me[1]
     Accept me[2]
      Call me the apple of Your eye[3]
      Your friend[4]
     Choose me[5]
      Love me[6]

Just
Amazes me!

[1] *Psalms 32:5*
[2] *Ephesians 1:6*
[3] *Zechariah 2:8*
[4] *John 15:15*
[5] *John 15:16*
[6] *Galatians 2:20*

Day 21

God's Love

What is
Unmatched?[1]
Unlimited?[2]
Unconditional?[3]

God's love for you and for me!

[1] *John 3:16*
[2] *Jeremiah 31:3*
[3] *Romans 5:8-10*

Day 22

Tonight

Me: Heavenly Father, as I lay my head down to sleep tonight, I place all my cares in Your hands: my family, friends, the past, the present, and the future.

Heavenly Father: Dearest daughter, I did not create you to worry. I am your Burden Bearer. I am your Help. Leave them all to Me. With them in My hands, you can rest.

Give all your worries and cares to God,
for He cares about you. ~ 1 Peter 5:7

Day 23

To Think

To Think

that You call me
beautiful[1]
created in Your image[2]
fearfully and wonderfully made[3]
special[4]
the apple of Your eye[5]
accepted[6]
chosen[7]
precious[8]
loved[9]
simply overwhelms me!

[1] *The Song of Solomon 6:4*
[2] *Genesis 1:27*
[3] *Psalms 139:14*
[4] *Deuteronomy 7:6*
[5] *Zechariah 2:8*
[6] *Ephesians 1:6*
[7] *John 15:16*
[8] *Isaiah 43:4*
[9] *Jeremiah 31:3*

Day 24

A Prayer for Today

Father,
help me
to never
look back
look down
look around
but always
look up
to You
because
You have
all the answers
to my life
Amen!

*I look up to the mountains—does my help come
from there? My help comes from the LORD, who
made heaven and earth! ~ Psalm 121:1-2*

*My soul, wait you only upon God; for my
expectation is from Him. ~ Psalm 62:5*

Day 25

A Brand New Day

Father, I thank You
for the beauty of a brand-new day
Another opportunity
to love and to be loved
to forgive and to be forgiven
to speak kind words
to hope
to dream
to expect
to fulfill
the plan that You have for my life.
In Jesus' name,
Amen!

Listen to my voice in the morning, Lord. Each morning I bring my requests to You and wait expectantly. ~ Psalm 5:3

Day 26

You Are

You are:
>Fearfully and wonderfully made.[1]

The apple of God's eye.[2]
>Precious and honored in His sight.[3]

Loved with an everlasting love.[4]
>Chosen before the creation of the

world.[5]

Created in His image.[6]
>Engraved on the palms of His hands.[7]

This defies human comprehension!

[1] *Psalm 139:14*
[2] *Zechariah 2:8*
[3] *Isaiah 43:4*
[4] *Jeremiah 31:3*
[5] *Ephesians 1:4*
[6] *Genesis 1:27*
[7] *Isaiah 49:16*

Day 27

May I Remind You

May I remind you?

"Whosoever trusts in Me, happy is he."[1]
"In all your ways acknowledge Me."[2]
"Pray without ceasing."[3]
"I will perfect that which concerns you."[4]
"I have chosen you."[5]
"My mercies are new every morning."[6]
"I will guide you with My eye."[7]
"I am great, and I do wondrous things."[8]
"I have called you by your name."[9]
"Every hair on your hair is numbered."[10]
"All things are possible with Me."[11]
"I will give you rest.[12]
With all My love, Jesus

[1] *Proverbs 16:20b* [2] *Proverbs 3:6*
[3] *1 Thessalonians 5:17* [4] *Psalm 138:8*
[5] *John 15:16b* [6] *Lamentations 3:23*
[7] *Psalm 32:8b* [8] *Psalm 86:10*
[9] *Isaiah 43:1* [10] *Matthew 10:30*
[11] *Matthew 19:26b* [12] *Matthew 11:28*

Day 28

My Life

Sometimes I think about the past
Missing the joy of the present
and the hope of the future.
Heavenly Father,
help me to enjoy each precious moment
of this life You have given me
O Lord,
my Hope[1]
my Strength[2]
my Peace[3]
my Creator.[4]

[1] *Psalm 71:5*
[2] *Psalm 19:14*
[3] *John 14:27*
[4] *Genesis 1:27*

Day 29

Special

The Psalmist David declares,
"How precious are Your thoughts about me,
O God! They cannot be numbered!
I can't even count them;
they outnumber the grains of sand!"[1]

It means that I am being thought about
by my Heavenly Father many more times
than I can number the sand.

Now, that really warms my heart
and makes me feel special!

[1]*Psalm 139:17-18a*

The Greatest Exchange

From: mourning to joy[1]
darkness to marvelous light[2]
ashes to beauty[3]
corruptible to incorruptible[4]
mortal to immortal[5]
weeping to joy[6]
eternal death to eternal life.[7]
The exchange that belongs to you and to Me!

[1] *Jeremiah 31:13;* [2] *1 Peter 2:9;* [3] *Isaiah 61:3;*
[4,5] *1 Corinthians 15:53; Psalm 30:5;* [7] *John 3:16*

Questions

Heavenly Father, my questions are always the same. Do I deserve Your love? Do I deserve Your forgiveness? Do You really understand what I have done?

Dearest daughter, My answer to you is always the same. My love for you is everlasting.[1] I forgive you.[2] I know what you have done.[3] Nothing can ever separate you from My love.[4] Ask for My forgiveness.[5] Believe I have forgiven you.[6] Accept My forgiveness.[7] It is My gift to you.[8]

[1] *Jeremiah 31:3;* [2] *Psalm 103:3;* [3] *Psalm 69:19;*
[4] *Romans 8:38-39;* [5] *Psalm 51:1;* [6] *Isaiah 1:18;* [7] *John 8:11;*
[8] *Psalm 86:5*

About the Author

As a writer and speaker, Merle M. Mills, founder of *Changed Through The Word*, ministers throughout the Hampton Roads area sharing the good news of how words from the Holy Scriptures has changed her life to peace ... to joy ... to strength.

Her prayer is that her reading and listening audience will allow the power of the ever-living God the freedom to do the same in and through their lives.

Her book and accompanying CD, *No More A Secret*, bring hope and healing to women, especially those experiencing after-abortion trauma.

Merle resides with her family in Norfolk, Virginia.

Changed Through the Word
P. O. Box 41293
Norfolk, VA 23541

www.changedthrutheword.org
changedthrutheword@gmail.com
www.nomoreasecret.blogspot.com